Mum and Dad went camping.
They took the children.
They went to a farm.

Mum and Dad had a new tent.
They put it up.
Wilf helped.

Wilma got some water.
'I like it here,' she said.
'I like camping.'

Mr Jones was the farmer.
He had to milk the cows.
'Come and watch,' he said.

4

'What a lot of cows!' said Wilf.
Mr Jones laughed.
'We milk them every day,' he said.

Mum wanted some milk.
She went to the farm house.
'I want some eggs too,' said Mum.

Mrs Jones was expecting a baby.
She was expecting it soon.
'It may come today,' she said.

Dad cooked supper.
'I like it here,' said Wilf.
'It's fun in this tent.'

8

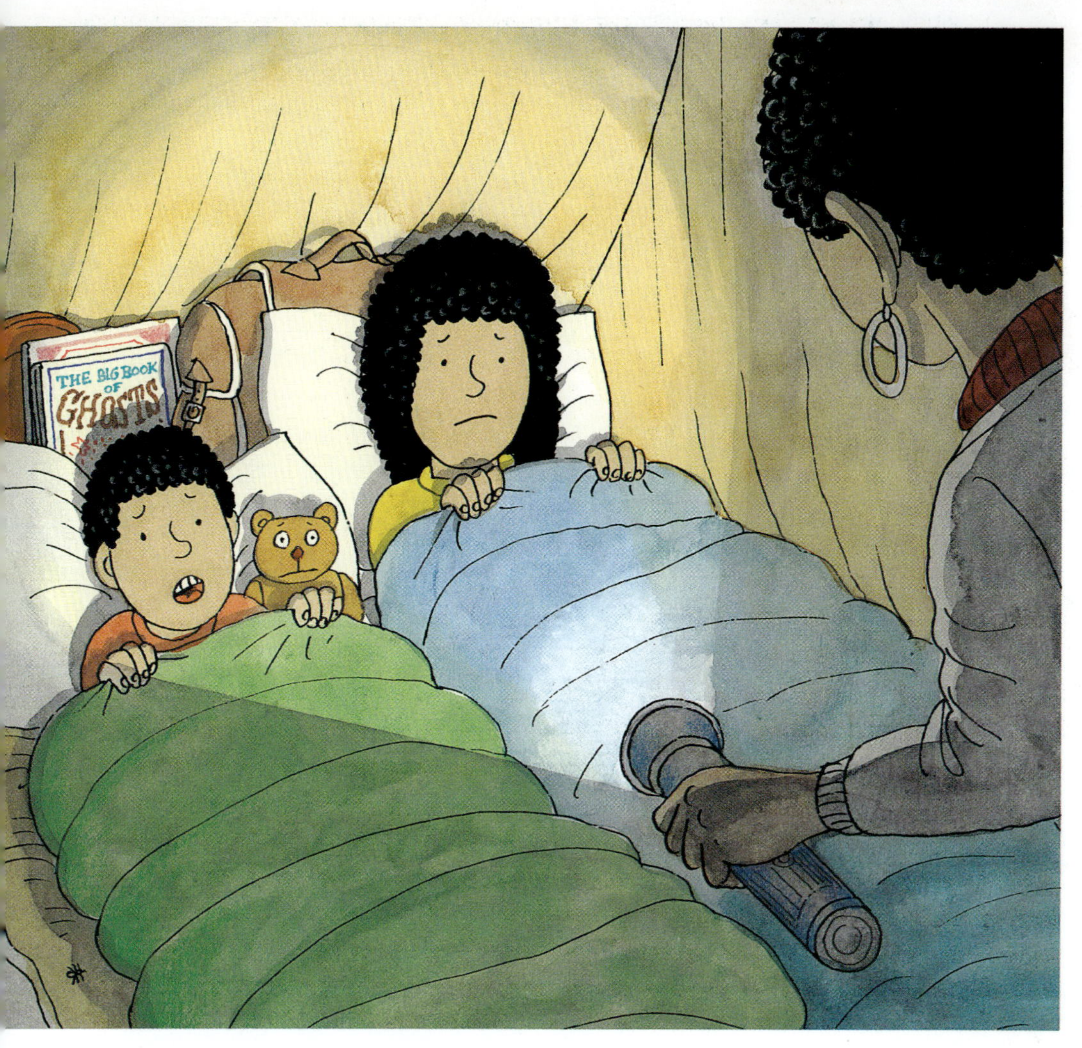

Everyone went to bed but
there was a storm.
Nobody could sleep.

The wind blew.
Everyone had to get up.

The wind blew the tent down.
They had to go to the farmhouse.

Mr Jones called Mum.
'The baby is coming,' he said.

Mrs Jones had to go to hospital.
She got in the car.
Mum helped her.

The storm got worse.
The wind blew and blew.
The wind blew a big tree down.

14

The car couldn't get past.
Mr and Mrs Jones went back to
the house.

Mr Jones called for help.
He called the hospital.
'A helicopter's coming,' he said.

Mr Jones pointed to a field.
'The helicopter can land there,' he said.

Mr Jones got some bags.
The children helped.
They got some big stones.

They made a big cross out
    of the bags.
They put stones on the bags.

The helicopter came.
It landed near the cross.
'At last!' said Mr Jones.

There was a doctor in
the helicopter.
'Come on!' said Mr Jones.

The doctor ran to the house but
Mum came to the door.
She was laughing.

22

'Too late!' said Mum.
'Mrs Jones has had the baby.
She's had a baby boy.'

Everyone looked at the baby.
'He's very sweet,' said Wilma.
'Will he like camping?'

24